Finding Your Place in
GOD'S GREAT STORY
for Little Ones

PAUL BASDEN & JIM JOHNSON

WITH KARI BASDEN DOBBS

ILLUSTRATIONS BY KYLE GAZZIGLI

HARVEST HOUSE PUBLISHERS
EUGENE, OREGON

God Creates

Ever since...well, forever, God the Father,
Jesus the Son, and the Holy Spirit have been
having a party in heaven.

God is love, and he has always loved us, so he wanted to invite as many people as possible to this party.

So he created humans and gave us a beautiful home—the earth.

God made billions of stars, plants, and animals,
and he asked us to take good care of everything.
God created the world, and God created you.
He delighted in all of creation.

Sadly, people began to sin and disappoint God. So he searched for someone who loved and followed him.

God Blesses

Many of God's children had turned away from him,
but Abraham loved and worshipped God.

God asked Abraham and his wife, Sarah, to move away from their home and family.

God also promised to give them a child.

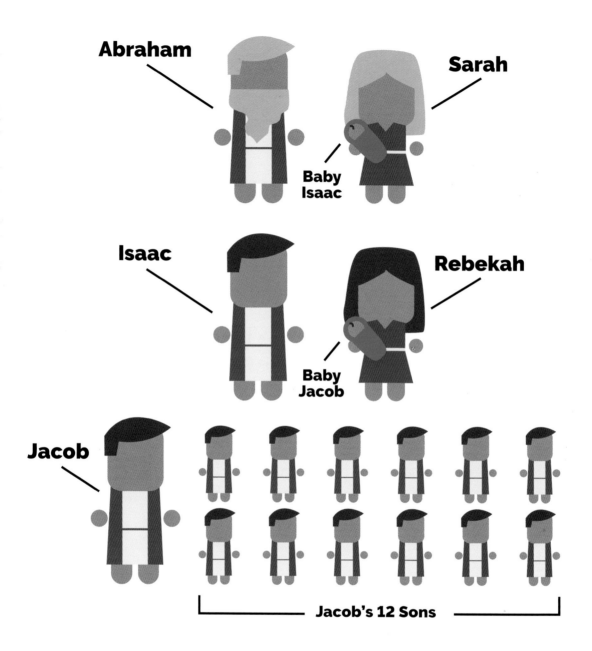

Abraham

Sarah

Baby Isaac

Isaac

Rebekah

Baby Jacob

Jacob

Jacob's 12 Sons

So they trusted God, and in their old age, God gave them a son named Isaac. Then Isaac had a son named Jacob. And Jacob had twelve sons who became the twelve tribes of Israel.

The Israelites were God's people,
and he would use them to bring light
to the dark world. God wants to bless
us so we can bless others.

God Rescues

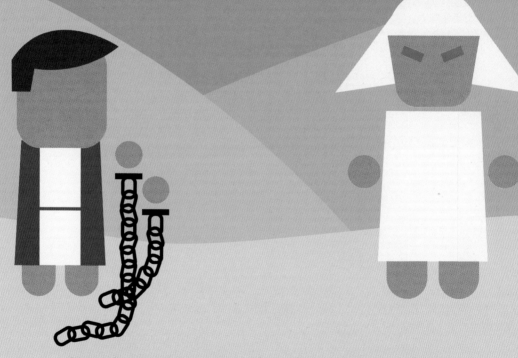

Jacob and his family moved to Egypt, but as their numbers grew, Pharaoh made them slaves and was mean to them.

Baby Moses

God's Plan

God had a special plan to rescue his people, and he called Moses to lead them. Even from birth, God had protected Moses from Pharaoh.

Adult Moses

One day while Moses was a shepherd in the desert, God spoke to him from a burning bush!

The Lord said,

Rescue my people, the Israelites, from slavery in Egypt.

HOLY GROUND

Please remove shoes

Moses was afraid, but he obeyed God and helped his people escape from Pharaoh.

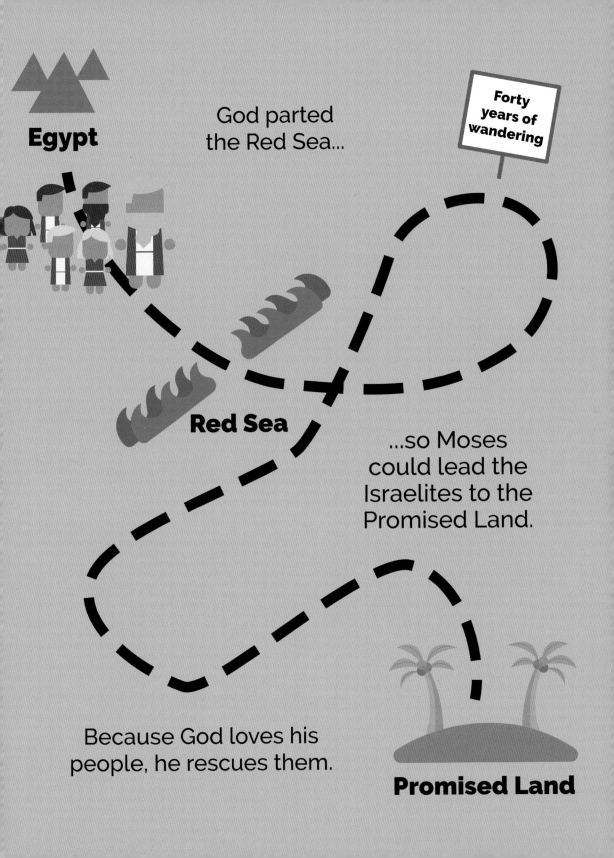

God Chooses

Sometimes the Israelites obeyed God,
but sometimes they didn't.

So God chose a faithful young shepherd
named David to be their king.

David trusted God with all his heart. He fought a giant named Goliath...

...and won because the Lord was on his side.

David wrote many beautiful songs for God.

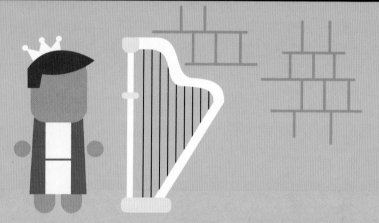

God made him a great warrior, and he led Israel with power and might.

David was not perfect though. He made some bad choices and sinned against God and others.

But David apologized to God and asked for forgiveness. God works with people who trust him and have humble hearts.

God Warns

Israel had many kings—some good, some bad. God loved his people very much. And he wanted them to love him back instead of worshipping other gods who weren't real.

So God sent prophets to warn Israel. The prophets reminded the Israelites how terrible life would be without God and how wonderful life would be with God.

God hoped the Israelites would listen and change their ways, but they didn't... and God's heart was broken.

God cared for his people, so he didn't give up. He decided to send someone even better than the prophets—his own Son, Jesus.

God Saves

God sent his only Son, Jesus, into our world through a young couple named Mary and Joseph.

When Jesus grew up, he began teaching people about God's love.

He performed miracles, like walking on water.

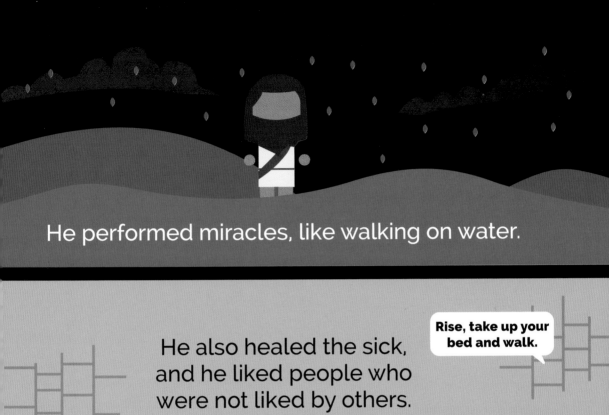

He also healed the sick, and he liked people who were not liked by others.

Rise, take up your bed and walk.

His best friends were called disciples.

Some people didn't understand Jesus.

They became jealous of his popularity, and they even killed him. He died on a cross and was buried.

But God brought Jesus back to life!
Because he loves us, Jesus gave his life to
save us from our sins and show us how to live.

God Sends

Jesus's disciples began sharing the good news all over the world: God raised Jesus from the dead!

God needed someone special
to lead this mission.
He chose Paul.

That was a surprise because Paul
had not been Jesus's friend before.

But God got Paul's attention with a bright light,
and Paul soon became Jesus's biggest fan.
Paul preached the good news,
and many people believed.

Paul faced many challenges. He even went to jail. But he praised God in every situation. God sent Paul around the world to tell people about Jesus. One day, no matter who you are, God can send you too.

God Wins

How does God's Great Story end?
God wins! The last book of the Bible is Revelation.
Jesus's disciple John wrote it to encourage his
friends who were going through hard times.

An angel gave him a vision of how one day Jesus
will come back to earth and make everything
perfect. Nobody will get sick or cry or die ever again.
Then we will be happier than we ever dreamed.

Jesus invites all of us to celebrate with him at a huge victory party. Everyone is invited, especially you. All you have to do is say *yes*!

Special thanks to
Kari Basden Dobbs,
who expertly edited this book
with her little ones in mind.

Cover and interior design by Dugan Design Group
Illustrations by Kyle Gazzigli

For bulk, special sales, or ministry purchases, please call 1 (800) 547-8979.
Email: Customerservice@hhpbooks.com

 This logo is a federally registered trademark of The Hawkins Children's LLC. Harvest House Publishers, Inc., is the exclusive licensee of this trademark.

ISBN 978-0-7369-8125-5 (hardcover)

Library of Congress Control Number: 2021947858

Printed in China

22 23 24 25 26 27 28 29 30 / LP / 10 9 8 7 6 5 4 3 2 1